Letter To My Great-Grandchild

Come and Listen, My Little One, to stories of when I was Young...

©2018 Traditions Press, Inc.

Lexington, South Carolina

ISBN-13: 978-1721161720

ISBN-10: 1721161724

Letter to My Great-Grandchild

Designed and illustrated by Nancy Simms Taylor

photo

Come and Listen,
My Little One,
And I will tell you stories
of when I was Young.

On a bench in the garden,
Or as we sit by the sea,
We have stories to share,
Just You and Me.

A Letter to My Great-Grandchild

photos

Great-Grandmother

(nickname)

_____

Full name

_____

Date and place of birth

_____

Her Parents

Mother _____

Born _____ Died _____

Occupation: _____

Father _____

Born _____ Died _____

Occupation: _____

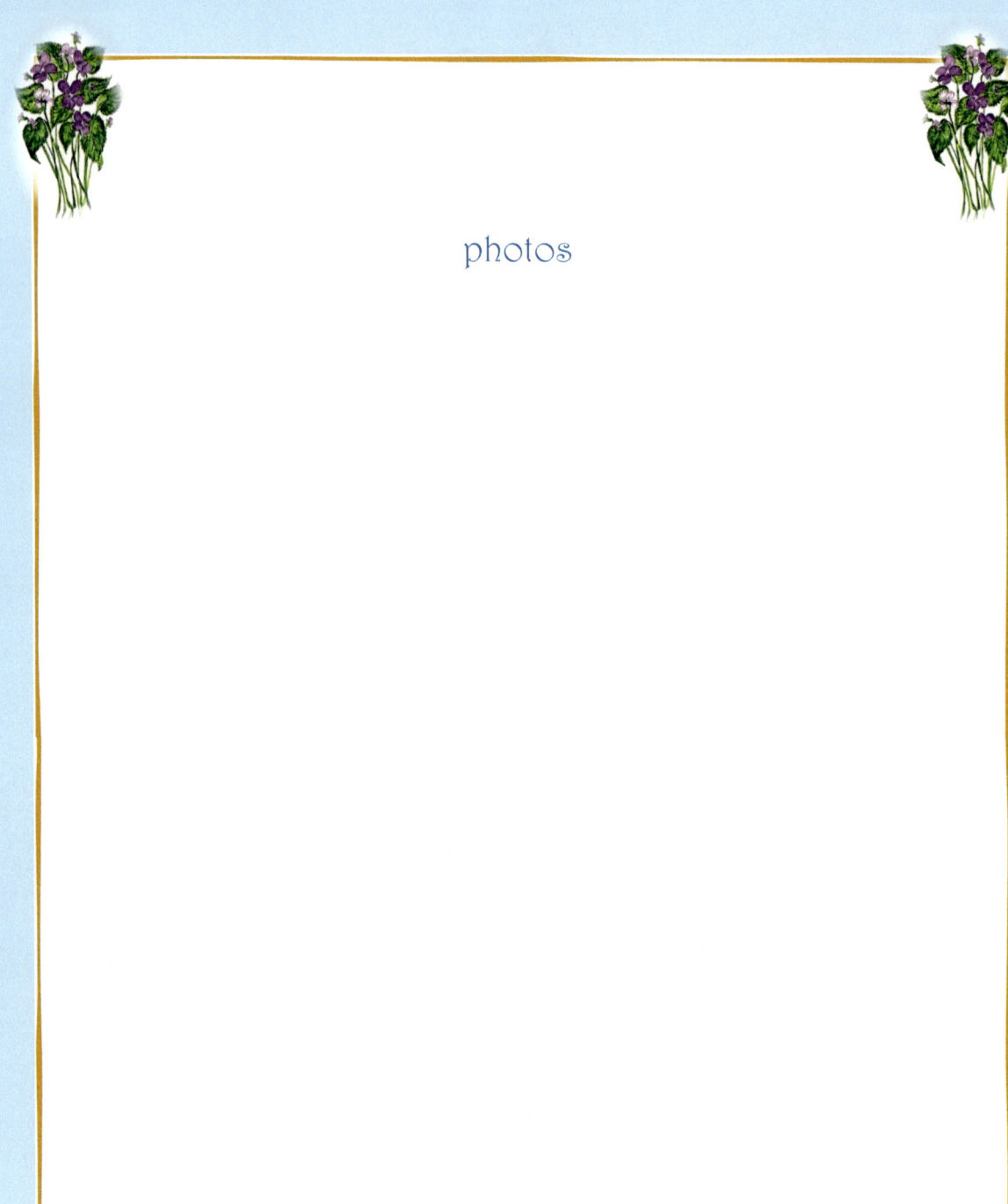

photos

Great-Grandfather

(Nickname) _____

Full name

_____

Date and place of birth

_____

His Parents

Mother _____

Born _____ Died _____

Occupation: _____

Father _____

Born _____ Died _____

Occupation: _____

Special Family Members and Friends

Family Traditions

Where I grew up and what life was like when I was a child...

Schooling

Elementary:

Middle:

High School:

And Beyond:

Activities and Hobbies

Spiritual Practices & Experiences

Favorite Places & Travels

People Who Inspired Me

My Favorite Foods

Recipe I want to share with you...

Inventions and Discoveries During My Lifetime

Major Historical Events During My Lifetime

Favorites

My favorite color _____

My favorite flower _____.

My favorite cookies are _____

Favorite Pet _____.

Favorite place to visit _____.

Best Friend_____

Favorite birthday_____

Favorite holiday_____

Favorite teacher _____

Favorite President _____

Other Favorites

_____

_____

_____

_____

Books, Movies & Entertainment from My Time

Favorite Movies

Favorite Television Shows

Favorite Songs

Favorite Books

-Favorite Artist

Words of Wisdom for my Great-Grandchild

Quote: _____
_____
_____
_____

Attributed to _____

Quote: _____
_____
_____
_____

Attributed to _____

Quote: _____
_____
_____
_____

Attributed to _____

Quote: _____
_____
_____
_____

Attributed to _____

Quote: _____
_____
_____
_____

Attributed to _____

Quote: _____
_____
_____
_____

Attributed to _____

Family Medical Information

Other Important Family Information

Family Stories

Photos & Mementos

Photos & Mementos

Photos & Mementos

Photos & Mementos

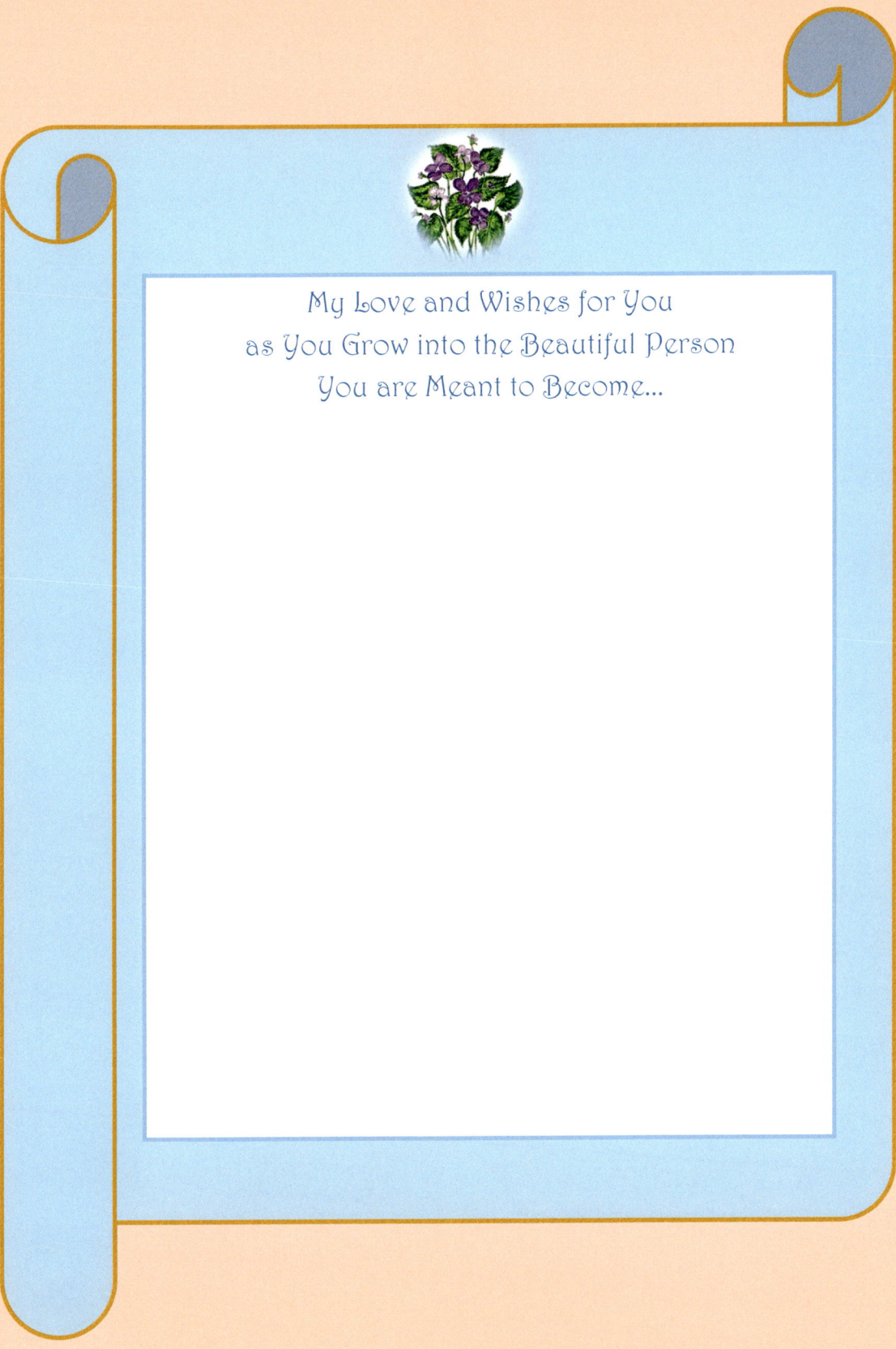

My Love and Wishes for You
as You Grow into the Beautiful Person
You are Meant to Become...

Made in the USA
Columbia, SC
28 January 2019